THE HEART

ALIVE™

A Practice of Moving from the Sex Center to the Heart Center

By Asttarte Deva

Author of The Heart On,

Opening the Heart of Your Beloved & Awaken to

Living, Tantra for Your Whole Life

THE HEART

ALIVE™

A Practice of Moving from the Sex Center to the Heart Center

By Asttarte Deva

The Heart Alive™, A Practice of Moving from the Sex Center to the Heart Center, by Asttarte Deva

Copyright 2023 by Asttarte Deva
ISBN Print Version: 979-8-9885137-4-2

Genre: Personal Growth/Tantra/Psychology

Second Edition, March 27, 2025

Cover by: Asttarte Deva

Published by: Asttarte Deva Publishing

Other Books by Asttarte Deva

Awaken to Living; Tantra for Your Whole Life

The Heart On; Opening The Heart of Your Beloved, Through Tantra, The Breath, The Art of Listening, Submission & Dominance in Intimate Relationships, A Guide for Couples & Tantra Healers.

Grieving the Shaman's Way; What I Learned from the Love of My Life Dying, On Healing the Shadow Side of a Relationship After Your Greatest Loss, With the Wisdom of Bufo the Toad, Spirit Medicine, Tantra, Intimacy, Breathwork & Being Our Authentic Selves

Grieving the Shamans Way Handbook; How To Get Over Your Grief in Four Months, With Breathwork, Meditation and Holistic Healing Practices

Asttarte's Meditation Program, From Basic Meditation to Advanced Tantra Meditation, A 4 Month Program

Other Books Asttarte is a Featured Author in:

How to Make Sacred Love to a Woman; An Intimate Exploration of Sacred Sexuality, by: Gabriel Morris

The Mystery of Woman; A Book for Men, by: Gabriel Morris

Recovering the Spirit; From Sexual Trauma; from the Traumatic to the Ecstatic, by: Kylie Devi

Dedicated to Paul my love

Contents

Preface

It was about 10 years ago when I decided I was ready to live out of my heart center. I knew there were limitations with only living from the pleasure center, and living a life of full body sexual orgasms all the time. Trust me, I could have continued my life living this way for the rest of my life. There was a lot of pleasure in it. I was happy most of the time, and I was numb to the fact that I didn't know how to fully receive or give love from my core. I didn't know any better. But, I knew somewhere deep inside that is what I ultimately wanted. I didn't know how I would accomplish this, but my deeper intuition, higher knowing and inner child showed me the way.

My boundaries started shifting in my work as a Sexual Healer. I started shifting from accepting any client, to having some restrictions. I screened people more thoroughly. I started saying No more, and I took more time to self-reflect, and meditate than ever before.

This bled into my personal life, and I started noticing that a lot of the people I was interested in dating also were mostly living out of their sex center. They were driven by their desire for orgasm, but they weren't driven for their desire for love. I started noticing how this affected my heart.

My heart cried for love, but all that kept showing up was sex. Sex was everywhere in my life. Sex was my drug. It was my poison and my spell. It drove me to help others with their own sexual challenges. It drove me to engage with certain people from my communities, and it determined a lot of my decisions. My creativity derived from my sex drive and passions. But I knew there was more.

As I continued on this journey and quest for attracting people who would truly love me for me, I started discovering that I too needed to learn to love me for me. And this began the journey of learning to love from within. Having grown up in a family where I didn't feel loved, this was quite a challenge to figure this out on my own. But I knew there was value here. I knew the significance and importance of self-love. I just couldn't grasp what it would look like and the journey I would go on to achieve it.

I started declining certain clients completely. And then, I started declining the men I had originally chosen to be intimate with. They misunderstood why I rejected them. But at my core, I knew they weren't capable of giving me the love I knew I truly deserved.

Then one day I met a student, who soon also became my teacher, and the love of my life. In teaching him all I could about Tantra, and working with the breath, energy healing, bodywork, and sexual intimacy, I discovered I could teach him how to bring his sexual energy up to his heart. And while I taught him how to do this, I practiced the same thing. We ended up becoming each other's Healers, as I wrote about in several other of my books.

This document, **The Heart Alive**ᴛᴍ, is the main ingredient for all of the work I talk about in many of my books. **The Heart On**, was originally going to be this specific practice, but that turned into an erotic tale and the personal story of some examples of how we worked together to achieve the mission of bringing the sexual energy up to the heart, through "Opening the Heart of Your Beloved". However, in that book, we talk mostly about the journey and the goal of being each other's support system and healers in the quest for healing the heart.

This book, **The Heart Alive**ᴛᴍ, is the origin, and the actual practice of moving up to the heart. Enjoy **The Heart Alive**ᴛᴍ. If you have questions, need support, or want to know how, reach out to me. I'd be happy to work with you.

Introduction

The Heart Alive™ is a practice for learning how to move from living in your root chakra, your sex center, up to your heart chakra, your heart center. Some people remain in one energy frequency their entire lives. They don't have the knowledge, awareness of how to shift it, or the desire or willingness.

With this book in your hands, if you truly desire to transform from living out of your sexual desires and going up to living from your heart, you can accomplish this. It is first the willingness, then the universe will bring you tools, people, and guidance to accomplish this.

You will have to go beyond just reading a book. You will need to sincerely practice the methods taught here to bring this home deeply into your heart. It will have to be a conviction. You must want really want it. Your drive to heal your heart will be your drive to fully *live in* your heart, and your goal of accomplishing it that much sooner.

The Heart Alive™ is your ticket home, but you hold the keys. And you must be the driver! You are in charge of your transformation and your path of awakening. At any point if you let someone else be the driver, they might be steering you in the wrong direction.

Its time now for our planet to evolve, and many of us are stepping up to support the collective journey of healing. Remember to listen to your heart, and let your inner wisdom be your teacher. When you give into your sexual cravings as your first place to ask questions or look for answers, you may always live in your sex center. But if you want to live out of your heart, truly feel self-love, heal your inner child, heal from any sex addictions, romantic obsessions, and stop jumping to your cravings, you must first take a breath, pause, and slow down.

We all learn from our mistakes, but instead of sabotaging yourself again, let's practice truly loving from within. Waking up the heart to feeling your whole heart and your whole self is the goal. Here is one path towards it.

1

What is The Heart Alive™?

The Heart Alive™ is a practice of going from the root chakra to the heart chakra. It is a method and way you can stop living out of your sexual center and find true love. The first path is on finding the love within and learning how to truly love yourself. Then you can share that love with others.

The Heart Alive™ is a practice of accessing your kundalini sexual energy and using it for healing the energy in your whole body and accessing your true heart. Many people are living out of their sex centers. Many are filled with heightened energies of sexual frustration, anger, disappointment, fear, sadness, and even control. **The Heart Alive**™ is a method of raising your vibration and consciousness and using that sexual energy you feel to heal your whole self.

We all experience sexual frustration at one moment or another. We all love the sensation of bliss, pleasure, and orgasm. **The Heart Alive**™ is like taking that sexual energy you feel at moments of bliss and using it to heal your core emotional self. At the height of your sexual arousal, you can take this sexual energy, and intentionally move it up the body to your heart center and allow it to support you to release all those emotions trapped in your body.

Many people who have heightened sexual energy feel frustrated by it. They don't know what to do with this strong sensation. They want to get rid of the sensation by having an ejaculation and release the pent-up energy right away. We're all human beings and its natural to want to have an orgasm with a release. However, when one does this quickly and right away, they are missing out on what working with this energy can offer you.

This is not the same as feeling the sensation and ignoring it. Some people choose to ignore it, or just don't have the time to put attention on it. However, for those who utilize this practice and work with their own sexual energy to heal their whole selves, especially their energetic and emotional selves, they have the chance to release a lot of trapped emotions in their bodies.

This method by itself, has a lot of keys to gold and assisting one to evolve and transform themselves. However, I often combine this with other methods I describe in some of my other books.

In this book, we will be covering the basics on **The Heart Alive**™ method, how you can add this practice to your regular meditation, and how you can add it to your intimate moments with your partner and grow as a couple together. This is also a method for anyone who wants to learn how to capture this profound practice to heal their own selves, while working with me, another practitioner, or on their own.

2

Why Practice The Heart Alive™?

Why is it important to practice **The Heart Alive™**? This is probably the most important question you are asking and is the reason for this book. Without knowing your why, you don't have motivation to do anything in life. The choices we make today affect our future, and if your why is big enough, you will find a way to do it.

All the top reasons to do the practice **The Heart Alive™**:

1. **Ejaculatory Control and a Healthy Sex Life**

Why Practice Ejaculatory Control for Men; what's all the fuss about?

- Improved sexual performance: Practicing ejaculatory control can lead to greater sexual satisfaction and improved performance during intercourse. Men may experience enhanced control over ejaculation, which can be particularly helpful for those dealing with premature ejaculation.

- Better prostate health: Regular pelvic floor exercises, which are often associated with ejaculatory control practices, can support prostate health and help prevent conditions like prostatitis and benign prostatic hyperplasia (BPH).

- Enhanced sexual health: Strengthening pelvic floor muscles through ejaculatory control exercises can improve blood flow to the pelvic area, potentially enhancing erection strength and duration.

- Stress reduction: Some practitioners report that ejaculatory control techniques can help reduce stress levels and promote relaxation.

- Potential boost to immunity: Some sources suggest that practicing sexual continence may stimulate the functioning of the immune system.
- Improved sleep quality: Ejaculatory control practices, combined with sexual activity, may lead to better sleep outcomes.

Ejaculatory control can enhance a man's sex life and positively impact his partner in several ways:

Benefits for Men:

- Energy Conservation: By retaining semen, men preserve their vital life force (Qi or Prana), leading to increased vitality and stamina.

- Multiple Orgasms: Mastering ejaculatory control allows men to experience orgasm without ejaculation, potentially leading to multiple orgasms.

- Spiritual Growth: Taoist and Tantric practices view sexual energy as a path to higher consciousness and spiritual enlightenment.
- Improved Sexual Function: Techniques like edging and pelvic floor exercises can help

address issues such as premature ejaculation and erectile dysfunction.

Benefits for Women

- Extended Pleasure: With improved stamina and control, men can engage in longer sexual sessions, allowing more time for female arousal and orgasm.

- Emotional Connection: Tantric practices emphasize mindfulness and emotional openness, fostering a deeper bond between partners.

- Multiple Orgasms: Taoist principles suggest that optimal sexual union involves multiple female orgasms.

Shared Benefits:

- Mutual Enjoyment: Prolonged intimacy allows both partners to explore new positions, techniques, and fantasies, keeping the experience exciting and fresh.

- Stronger Bond: Open communication about ejaculatory control creates trust and cooperation in addressing sexual concerns as a couple.

- Enhanced Intimacy: The focus on breath work, mindfulness, and energy circulation creates a more profound, intimate experience for both partners.

- Holistic Health: These practices are believed to contribute to overall well-being, including stress reduction and improved physical health.

By cultivating ejaculatory control, men can improve their sexual performance and deepen the physical and emotional connection with their partner.

Ejaculatory control is not just about physical technique but involves a holistic approach to sexuality, incorporating breath work, meditation, and energy cultivation practices. It's seen as a way to transform sexual energy into a more subtle, circulating form that can benefit both partners physically, emotionally, and spiritually.

Sex Addiction Recovery – for men and women

Men That are Oversexed

Recovering from sex addiction can offer numerous benefits for men and is a positive step towards overall well-being. Here are some key reasons why healing from sex addiction is beneficial:

Improved Mental Health

Sex addiction recovery can lead to significant improvements in mental health:

- Reduced anxiety and depression associated with compulsive sexual behaviors

- Increased emotional stability and better stress management

- Enhanced self-esteem and self-worth as shame and guilt diminish

Healthier Relationships

Overcoming sex addiction can greatly benefit personal relationships:

- Rebuilding trust with partners and family members

- Developing deeper, more meaningful connections
- Improved communication skills and emotional intimacy

Personal Growth

The recovery process often catalyzes substantial personal development:

- Greater self-awareness and understanding of one's needs and motivations

- Development of healthy coping mechanisms for stress and emotional challenges

- Increased productivity and focus on personal and professional goals

Physical Health Benefits

Addressing sex addiction can lead to improved physical health:

- Reduced risk of sexually transmitted infections

- Better overall sexual function as compulsive behaviors decrease

- Improved sleep patterns and general well-being

Enhanced Quality of Life

Recovery from sex addiction can result in a more fulfilling life:

- More time and energy for hobbies, interests, and personal relationships

- Increased sense of control over one's life and choices

- Greater alignment with personal values and life goals

Professional Improvement

Overcoming sex addiction can positively impact one's career:

- Increased focus and productivity at work

- Reduced risk of professional consequences related to addictive behaviors

- Improved decision-making skills in all areas of life

Healing from sex addiction is a transformative journey that can lead to a more balanced, fulfilling, and authentic life. It allows men to regain control, rebuild relationships, and rediscover their true selves beyond the constraints of addiction.

Women that are oversexed

Women that have a heightened sex drive, discomfort in her sex center all the time and cannot wait to have sex with many partners. Women that need to have sex with her significant partner all the time and an inability to be patient with when he wants to be sexual.

Overcoming sex addiction can be immensely beneficial for women's mental health and overall well-being. Here are some key benefits:

Mental Health Improvements

- Reduced anxiety and depression associated with compulsive sexual behaviors

- Increased emotional stability and better stress management

- Enhanced self-esteem and self-worth as shame and guilt diminish

- Improved ability to form healthy emotional connections

Relationship Benefits

- Rebuilding trust with partners and family members

- Developing deeper, more meaningful connections

- Improved communication skills and emotional intimacy

- Healthier boundaries in personal and professional relationships

Personal Growth

- Greater self-awareness and understanding of one's needs and motivations

- Development of healthy coping mechanisms for stress and emotional challenges

- Increased productivity and focus on personal and professional goals

- Improved decision-making skills in all areas of life

Regarding women with heightened sexual drives or discomfort:

Women experiencing persistent genital arousal or hypersexuality may face significant challenges in their daily lives and relationships. This condition can manifest as:

- Constant physical discomfort or arousal in the genital area

- An overwhelming desire for sexual activity that interferes with daily functioning

- Difficulty maintaining healthy relationships due to excessive sexual demands

- Emotional distress from the inability to control sexual urges

- Engaging in risky sexual behaviors with multiple partners

These women may struggle with:

- Maintaining focus on work or other responsibilities

- Experiencing shame or guilt about their sexual thoughts and behaviors

- Difficulty finding satisfaction in sexual encounters

- Strain on their primary relationships due to constant sexual demands

- Emotional exhaustion from the persistent state of arousal

Overcoming these challenges through therapy, support groups, and potentially medication can lead to a more balanced and fulfilling life, allowing women to regain control over their sexuality and form healthier relationships.

However, with the practice shared in the book, **The Heart Alive**™, women can in time heal the core of these issues and the added recommendations to help.

Doing the practice of The Heart Alive™ for Healing the Inner Child

Doing the practice of **The Heart Alive**™ can help to heal the inner child. It can help tap into the inner self and feelings that stem from early years of not feeling loved, not being able to receive love in a safe way, not receiving enough love as a young child and not feeling safe to give love in return.

When doing the practice of this breathing practice **The Heart Alive**™, all the feelings that are dormant from within, from a younger age, and the emotions that are unblocked can start to unpack in the process, especially when doing this practice with a partner that loves you deeply. Doing the practice with another can allow for the feelings of safety to be experienced that you may not have experienced previously. It is a life altering experience when you can do this over time and stick to it until you finally start to realize the feelings and emotions that have been there all along.

Doing the practice of The Heart Alive™ for Self-Love

The Heart Alive™ practice is a powerful method for cultivating self-love and healing the core of oneself. This practice offers a unique approach to personal growth and transformation by harnessing sexual energy and redirecting it for holistic healing.

Why Practice The Heart Alive™ for Self-Love
Integrating Mind, Body, and Spirit

The Heart Alive™ method helps individuals become fully integrated and whole within themselves. By moving energy from the root chakra to the heart chakra, it creates a bridge between our primal instincts and our capacity for love and compassion.

Transcending Sexual Frustration

Many people experience sexual frustration or feel overwhelmed by their sexual energy. The Heart Alive™ practice offers a constructive way to channel this energy, transforming it from a source of frustration into a powerful tool for healing and self-discovery.

Emotional Release and Healing

This practice facilitates the release of trapped emotions in the body. By intentionally moving sexual energy to the heart center, practitioners can access and process deep-seated emotions such as anger, fear, sadness, and disappointment.

Raising Consciousness

The Heart Alive™ method is not just about managing sexual energy; it's about raising one's vibration and consciousness. This elevated state of awareness can lead to profound insights and personal growth.

Finding True Love Within

By focusing on self-love and inner healing, practitioners learn to stop seeking fulfillment solely through external relationships. This practice helps individuals discover the love within themselves, which is essential before sharing love with others.

Holistic Approach to Sexuality

Rather than ignoring or quickly releasing sexual energy, **The Heart Alive™** encourages a more mindful and holistic approach. This can lead to a deeper understanding and appreciation of one's sexuality.

Enhancing Intimate Relationships

When practiced with a partner, **The Heart Alive**™ can foster growth and deeper connection in relationships. It encourages open communication and shared spiritual experiences.

Personal Empowerment

Learning to work with one's own sexual energy for healing and transformation is deeply empowering. It gives individuals tools to take charge of their emotional and spiritual well-being.

The Heart Alive™ practice offers a unique path to self-love and personal transformation. By harnessing the power of sexual energy and directing it towards healing and heart-centered awareness, individuals can experience profound changes in their emotional, spiritual, and relational lives.

With the combined reasons to do the practice **The Heart Alive**™, between Ejaculatory Control for men, Sex Addiction Recovery for men, Sex Addiction Recovery for women, Healing the Inner

Child and Self-Love, doing this practice is a crucial part of one's journal and personal growth.

3

How to Practice The Heart Alive™

How to Practice **The Heart Alive**™ first starts with a recognition. The first step is simply having awareness that you are feeling your sexual energy. You may want to take care of business if you truly cannot handle the frustration, but if you truly want to learn the practice of bringing that sexual energy up to your heart, pause before you take care of things, and wait.

Now if you are reading this book and you don't have a heightened sexual energy, but you see the value in working with your sexual energy to help achieve another level of Ascension and Enlightenment, this practice is also for you. For those interested in doing this practice to achieve Ascension, release emotions trapped out of your body, heal your inner child, awaken your kundalini and manifest a partner in your life, this practice is also for you. Yes, you will awaken your Kundalini through this practice. You will also tap into your inner child. This practice will give you an opportunity to process the feelings you have trapped inside of you.

This is not your typical breathing practice or Tantra practice!

Here is the recipe for those who want to work on transforming their inner self to a place of balance, live more out of their heart center, heal their inner child and manifest a partner into your life.

Step 1: Find a comfortable place to lay down in private without distractions. Chose if you want to do the practice solo or with a partner.

Step 2: Pause

Step 3: Take a breath

Step 4: Close your eyes and go within

Step 5: Notice your whole body. Become aware of your body.

Step 6: Place your hands on your heart

Step 7: Set your intention of what you want to open or let go of

Step 8: Begin to squeeze your genital muscles, breathe in with the squeeze and hold in the squeeze on the inhale. Continue holding in the breath. Count to 5 or 6 on the inhale squeeze. If you are able to hold the breath for 10 to 15 seconds that is even better. Work up to this. Hold the breath, visualize the energy going up to your heart and then exhale.

Step 9: Continue this practice of inhaling up to the heart on the inhale and squeezing, working up to 15 seconds of holding the breath and squeeze.

Step 10: Repeat until you start to feel emotions rising up in you.

Step 11: It may take continuing the practice 3 times a week for 3 weeks to start feeling the emotions stir up. For those with stubborn armor and energy around their body it will take longer.

Step 12: Continue the practice even after emotions rise to the surface for about an hour at each Session. For those determined folks who are ready to release all the emotions trapped in their bodies, you can go longer than an hour. At this point it will be helpful to have a partner by your side or a guide.

Step 13: Continue this practice for a minimum of six months of doing the practice continuously. At this point, you will be able to support others.

Step 14: Repeat from Step 1! Do not stop your own practice! Keep going. Keep releasing, and eventually you will manifest a partner to do this with. First you must work on releasing the emotions inside of you.

Ascension is possible!

Steps for those who want to shift their heightened sexual energy to balance:

Step 1: Pause

Step 2: Take a breath

Step 3: Close your eyes, and go within.

The energy may be really high. It may feel extremely uncomfortable. You may have the urge to self-pleasure right away or find a partner to help you to release the arousal or discomfort. Before you release the energy, wait. Whether you are male, or female does not make a difference.

If you are in a relationship, it may actually be easier to practice this method, but it can still be done alone. As experiences and moments in life trigger your arousal, you can come back home within and do your practice.

Step 4: Set your intention of what you want to work on, or let go of

Step 5: Take a moment and feel all of your body. With your eyes still closed, feeling the heightened sexual energy, breathe into this energy. Take deep breaths. Notice how strong the sensation is. Continue breathing.

Step 6: Place your hands over your heart. Set the intention to pull the sexual energy up to your heart. Breathe deeply into it again.

Step 7: With your inhale, breathe into your sexual organs and sexual center. With your exhale, visualize the energy going up to your heart. Imagine your heart opening like a flower, as big and wide as the sun.

Step 8: Keep your eyes closed. Imagine your own energy expanding, lifting, rising up to your heart. Continue noticing it. Continue breathing into it.

Step 9: You will start to feel pulses in your genitals, or tension, begin to squeeze your genital muscles, breathe in with the squeeze and hold in the squeeze. Continue holding in the breath. After 5 to 6, even up to 10 seconds of holding the squeeze and holding the breath, exhale and visualize the energy going up to your heart.

It may feel challenging at this point.

Step 10: Be aware of your body and what your body is feeling. Continue breathing deeply. Breathe in your nose and out your mouth. If you have a partner with you, ask him or her to place their hands over your heart. Ask them to hold you and cuddle you while you're breathing.

All you're doing at this point is breathing, and noticing your intense sexual energy. The sexual energy is showing you something. It's showing you something you need to heal within yourself.

Step 11: Continue squeezing your sexual muscles and pulling the energy up. At this point you may get emotional. You may start to feel anger. Breathe into the anger. Notice it. Just become aware, like you're an angel watching over yourself, witnessing your feelings.

Continue breathing into the feelings. As you continue breathing, you may feel sadness. Just keep breathing. Continue squeezing and continue feeling whatever it is your body is feeling. If tears come, let them. Just keep breathing, holding presence, squeezing when you can, and exhaling the energy.

As you continue the practice, you may feel more feelings. You may feel deeper sensations. Just continue the practice. You may notice your kundalini. Just become aware. Be the witness to your own process.

Step 12: Notice how your heart feels. Notice how it expanded. Notice a sensation of love for yourself greater than before. If you're with a partner, notice how you can feel his or her love bigger than before. Witness how they too, can feel love coming from you bigger than before. This practice may open your partners heart too. Don't be surprised.

If you're alone, just continue the breathing and noticing. Wrap your arms around yourself, or perhaps grab a pillow and hold it to your chest. Continue breathing in the energy up to your heart. Continue feeling the sensations, energy, and emotions you are feeling.

Keep breathing, keep squeezing, and keep giving yourself love.

I'll go further into this practice throughout this book and explain how to use the method in different situations and experiences.

You got this!

4

The Heart Alive™ Alone

Practicing **The Heart Alive™** individually is a different experience than practicing it with a partner. It may be more challenging to practice it alone at first. You may feel you deeply need another person to share the experience with, share sexual energy with, and just to be held by them. Over time it does get easier to practice this method on your own. You have less struggle to just settle into the energy.

In time, you can begin to master understanding your own sexual energy and how to harness it as a practice for self-love. When you are alone, you may deeply feel that you need to release the sexual energy right away. However, remember, this only releases the frustration. It does not cause purification of the emotional self, unless you combine the practice of **The Heart Alive**™, and bring the energy up to your heart for some time, and then afterwards, do your self-pleasure release practice. However, sometimes after you've worked with the sexual energy for emotional healing, you might discover the sexual tension disappears too. Often, the orgasm actually wants to release emotional tears, and when the tears come out of the eyes, often the same kundalini energy has been released, but from a different part of yourself.

It's like the sex center having an orgasm out of the heart when the eyes tear. When you can feel the love for yourself, and you cry the emotional tears that need to be released, the sexual tension goes away. Love remains, and bliss is expanded.

It's not crucial to pull the sexual energy up to your heart every single time, but in order to truly heal where your energy lives the majority of the time and to bring it up to the heart, it is important to continue this practice when you feel the energy arise.

For those who have lived in their sex center most of their lives, who have been tempted by others sexuality, and are used to getting their needs met immediately, this practice may be harder for you. But it can be done. You have the power to choose how to act on these cravings, and how you want to respond to the world around you. Every human being has the capacity to heal their sexual energy. Even if you've been living in a high sexual energy your entire life, you can still learn how to bring the energy up to your heart.

This practice often works better after you've had a rise in your energy from interacting with someone you felt an energy with, either on the phone or in person, or even in other ways. Some people feel a rise even over text from people. However, when the chemical hormones of arousal ignite their pleasure zones and they feel stimulated in their root center after an energy exchange, this is the best time to do this practice.

Some people can feel an arousal after thinking about someone. They may feel that energy lift in their sex center just from their mind and the thoughts they think about someone there may be a strong pull to be with. This is also a good time to do this practice.

You are still alone doing this technique, so you get the benefits of filling yourself up with your own love and using your own love energy to heal your heart. You can choose to engage and interact with this person later, and show them this practice. In the beginning, while you are learning, you may want to choose to be intentional to fully heal your sex energy and fully heal your heart before sharing your sexual energy with another.

You may want to choose to only be with others for true love, or when you feel your heart has fully (or mostly) healed. If so, the solo practice is very important. That is always a personal choice.

This is an opportunity to fully love yourself at your core. You can choose to do this practice until you have completely healed all of your heart, all your internal wounds, emotional pains, blocks, traumas, and sometimes it's nice to have someone be a mirror to help reflect back what you still have left to work through inside yourself. That is a personal preference. Everyone has the right to choose what's right for them.

You can also use this practice alongside your discovery of learning about yourself and the way your energy responds to those you interact with, friends, loved ones, or sexual interests. You can use it alongside your gentle dating experiences, or if you are currently in a committed partnership. You can do this **The Heart Alive**™ practice alone, and when you re-engage with your loved one, teach them this practice and do it together, or continue to do the practice every time you separate from your partner and feel the sexual urge rise up inside of you.

I recommend you do it the way it works best for you.

I also recommend do it the way you will experience the most amount of sexual stimulation, so you can use this practice to pull the sexual energy up and work through the deep feelings that have been wanting to come up. The more you experience the heightened arousal, the more you have a chance to do this practice and do it in a way that will help you to transform the energies inside of you.

When sexual energy is at a high, it is your bodies wisdom telling you there is an emotion that wants to be released. You don't have to be scared of the energy. You don't have to avoid it. And you don't need to get rid of it quickly either. It's your internal energy and it's a message that there's an emotion that wants to come up.

Be curious. Don't assume you know what it is. Allow yourself to wonder and surrender to this energy. Be with it. Breathe with it. Drop into the energy like you would a meditation. Let yourself fully feel it. See it as a test, a challenge, to go deeper into your soul. It is there for you to teach you and help you heal and become the greatest version of yourself.

It is also there to bring you bliss, joy and pleasure. You have an opportunity to experience full body orgasm and pleasure with this energy, with your breath and your body alone. You don't need anyone's approval to experience this. You don't need to ask permission. And you don't need to do it with anyone else, unless you really want to of course. If you can do it with yourself, and fully love yourself and heal your heart, then yes, of course you can do it with others too. You may end up becoming their healer or teacher by doing so, and that's a good thing.

If it's a challenge for you to do it alone, if you feel scared, sad, lonely, or fear, you may want to do it with a partner. But experiment with yourself and do it alone first. See if you *can* do it alone. You may feel a deep sense of loneliness that is inside, or feelings of abandonment, isolation, or rejection. If these feelings are there, it may be difficult to do it alone, but you can try. Breathe into these feelings. They want to heal and leave. They don't want to be there forever. They are showing up because they want to be released out of your energy and body. All you need to do is notice them. Close your eyes, breathe into the feelings, do your Heart Alive practice, squeezing your genitals and pulling that energy up to your heart, and see what happens.

Working with pillows, blankets or stuffed animals is really helpful. I know you might be thinking, "what is this she's talking about?" But trust me, this is in fact inner child healing work. The little girl or boy inside of you will be really happy you used these props and did this for them. You will be healing that little you inside of you just a little bit at a time each time you do this.

You may start off this practice with having a lot of armor around your body. And after months or years of doing this, you'll notice how much lighter you are and the pure innocent beautiful being that you are. It takes time to remove layers of protection you've put around yourself since you were a child. But as the layers lift, and you start to feel more and more connected to your heart, you'll notice how much happier you are on the inside. Rushing to respond to stimulations or get rid of the sensation of arousal or sexual frustrations will lessen over time. You won't need to rush. You'll be able to be more present with each experience. You'll find yourself feeling more love for yourself than ever before. And in that presence, you'll feel more peace.

5

The Heart Alive™, Honoring Your Heart & Protecting Your Energy

When you take the path of honoring your heart, such as the path of rising out of the dominant sexual life force and the heart begins to open and blossom over time, sexual urges and needs to be spontaneous and impulsive becomes less. You start to see the value in leading from your heart. You start taking your time and being more patient with your experience as a human. Most especially you become more patient on the path and quest of connecting to others energy and experiencing a love connection with other people.

You start to see the value in being more selective with those you engage with and being more careful with who you choose to get close to. You begin to see the value in taking your time. You don't let just anyone's energy blend with yours.

You realize your value, your worth, and how important you are. And seeing your heart as sacred becomes more important to you. Sexual urges become less. They may still be there, but you start to notice that honoring your true heart is more important than your sexual cravings. For those who are married or in a significant partnership, you may begin to see that your boundaries, needs, and requests are just as important as your partners. And, in fact, you may start to honor your own self more.

When you honor your heart in this beautiful way, you also start to see that those you chose to surround yourself with also may become more selective. You may become more selective with your friends or begin to set limits with certain individuals. You may no longer tolerate certain behaviors, and either pull back from certain people, openly communicate that their behaviors don't sit well with you or limit the amount of time you spend with them and the frequency.

This also may begin to bleed over to your clients as well, and those you serve and spend quality time with, in private session or healing packages may become more important that these individuals also are aligned with your true intentions and soul purpose. Clients that are not in alignment with your purpose, your truth, your values, and beliefs are just as important as though you are selecting them to be a significant partner in your life. If the compatibility is missing, it does not mean there is something wrong with either of you. It just means you are not a fit to work together.

As your frequency raises, your integrity for truth and the heart goes to a higher place of sincerity, the types of people you are attracted to and who are attracted to you will shift and change. When we keep our heart open for all people and all types, no matter who they are and they don't align with who we are, it can cause a rift in our auric field and our soul. It may take us or them down a path that may cause more harm to who we are than we realize. Trusting in your inner wisdom is crucial in the matters of the heart, your energy and protecting the beautiful person you have become. The more you work on yourself and know your worth the more important this becomes.

6

The Heart Alive™ in Relationships

When you're in a relationship with a loved one, the practice of **The Heart Alive™** is so helpful and beneficial. It can turn a casual relationship into something beautiful and profound, and a relationship suffering to something extremely close and a deeper understanding and love for the other. You have the added benefit of doing the practice with a partner who knows you deeply, and you have an opportunity to go that much deeper because you have someone by your side.

When you're dating and just getting to know your partner, and you bring in **The Heart Alive**™ practice with your partner, you learn things about each other that only makes sense that you would want to get to know each other much more. **The Heart Alive**™ in a dating relationship can bring compassion, understanding, support, caring, and kindness where it didn't exist before.

How you practice **The Heart Alive**™ exercise in a dating relationship, may be more subtle, gentle, and cautious than it would be in a more significant partnership. You're still just getting to know each other. You may not be ready to go to such a depth of wanting to witness all your partners vulnerabilities or deeper feelings. Maybe you're still in the putting on a good face phase of your relationship and you want your partner to see all the good qualities you have, rather than your weaknesses. This is understandable. However, if you take the risk, and do show your vulnerabilities, you may be surprised at how much closer you become.

Trust begins to build, and a greater appreciation will grow. You may start to feel safer with your relationship as you surrender to each other and melt in the unknown. With each inhale you take in your kundalini and heart practice, you shed more and more layers that are covering up who you really are. A greater love begins to exist that you perhaps may not have imagined prior to this experience. And a love for self grows even stronger.

7

The Heart Alive™ in Marriages

The Heart Alive™ in Marriages is one of the most profound ways of utilizing this practice. You have a unique and golden opportunity to work on your core self, your hidden and shadow self. You get to shine and blossom in the process of doing this practice with a committed partner by your side.

You don't necessarily have to do it every time with your partner, or even in the same room. But the benefits of doing it this way reap rewards you won't even recognize until weeks, months and sometimes years later of continuing the practice.

Your sexuality and drive are the leader that causes this manifestation, but your heart, body and soul reap the benefits.

A marriage with the added benefit of including this powerful tantra meditation and breathwork practice will slowly over time, become closer and more powerful than ever before. As you continue the practice with your Beloved, you will begin to see how it helps to unfold what is necessary to remove blocks in the way of your intimacy. You will gain confidence, feel more secure with how you feel and begin to express your truth to your partner. The vulnerability you share will allow a closeness you may have not experienced before.

As you breathe with your partner, surrender in their arms, or beside them, you will expand your capacity to feel each other, and yourselves. There is nothing you need to do other than to breathe. And you can also make requests of your Beloved since you have already established a secure closeness with the other. The more you breathe, the more you remove what's in the way to be genuine with your feelings and who you are.

There's no pretending when you do this practice with your Beloved. There's no hiding. You cannot put on a fake show and pretend to feel a certain way or behave a certain way when your true vulnerabilities arise. You get confronted with who you really are, and how you truly feel.

With your Beloved, you are the Witness, and you are also being witnessed. You experience a level of being with your partner that is like the experience of oneness. Your genuine self shows.

As the Witness

With you as the witness to your partner, you get to experience your partner for who he or she truly is. You can hold space and be present with him/her. You can lay together and be supportive in whatever way you feel your partner needs. As the witness, you are his/her Healer. You are the space holder. You are your partners Shaman, Coach and Beloved. You are also their mirror. When you continue to hold space in this way, they may be confronted with being witnessed, and also recognize that what you are seeing may be scary or difficult for them. There's nothing to be afraid of. It's just their true feelings. The emotions that arise will eventually clear, and settle into their system, but if at any point they have trouble or are struggling, just continue to breathe with them. All you have to do is breathe. Eventually the feelings move through them. And you will feel it too, as the two of you are interconnected. When your partners energy settles, you will melt and relax too.

If at any point it is too much for you, you feel overwhelmed, overstimulated, triggered, or you become tired or need to take a break, you can communicate that whenever it shows up for you. This is not your job. This is your Beloved, and the most important thing to maintain closeness and trust is to be honest and express the truth, as often as you can. When you keep things to yourself, over time, resentment can build, and walls can become built, and then the closeness lessens as inauthenticity grows. Be honest and tell the truth and your love will grow.

As the one Being Witnessed

When you are the one being witnessed, you get to relax. You're clocking out now, and there's no work you need to do. Instead of being the space holder, you are the one who let's go of control, let's go of the reins and surrenders in the process of being witnessed. Your partner also may not have much to do other than observe your experience. However, when you have a need, or a request, you have a chance to do that at this time.

When you are in your process, in your experience, you also have the choice if you want your partner to stay alongside you the entire time, or if you need time alone. You can choose to take some time alone, and when you are ready to be witnessed again, request your partner to return to your sacred healing station the two of you started from.

When you are the one being witnessed, you are the one who is the most vulnerable. If you have trauma that is coming up, old hurts, griefs, resentments, disappointments, shame, sadness, fear, regret, or anything else, you are vulnerable. It's important to share what's coming up for you but do it at your pace. If you are not ready to talk about it, that's ok. You can ask to be held and continue to breathe together. You can slow down the breathing as it gets to be a lot and choose to slow down the practice and come to an end, or resume the practice after some time of rest.

Just remember, as the one being witnessed you are always in charge of your process. You get to say how much you can handle and how deep you want to go, and how quickly. No one is forcing you to do this deep work, but you will grow and become a better version of you as you do.

8

The Heart Alive™ and Sharing Love

The practice of **The Heart Alive™** can become an extraordinary opportunity for sharing love with others and yourself. When your heart is wide open you want to share that love with others. However, sometimes we may want to share love with others who are not ready to receive it. This can end up hurting our own hearts if you put too much energy into giving. However, we also don't want to guard our hearts too much and keep a distance from others from experiencing connection, love, and the beauty of sharing.

It's important to keep a healthy balance, find harmony and allow your heart to be receptive to receiving the love it so deserves. Sometimes we need to do more giving than receiving for a time when others struggle with allowing love in, are afraid, protect themselves, or don't know how to trust another's love.

Don't take it personally when another cannot receive the love you have to give. They just may not be ready to experience that deep closeness. Everyone opens their hearts at their own time and their own pace. However, if it causes you pain to wait for another to open to you, be kind to yourself and don't wait and suffer along with them. They may want you to wait. You can wait as best as you are able, but be sure to receive love where you need it and in the way that suits you best.

9

The Heart Alive™ for Hormonal Balance

The Heart Alive™ practice for balancing the hormones, is just like the other Tantra Meditation practices I talk about in some of my other books. However, the difference with this practice, is the energy is just going up to the heart, instead of down and out the body as in other practices.

Breathing your sexual energy up to your heart can be balancing and harmonizing when you are feeling a peak of hormonal release, chemical imbalances, brain fog, depression, anxiety, anger, or irritability, an extreme of arousal or even during moments of added heat and sweating during peri-menopause or menopause. It can help reduce hormonal or peri-menopausal/menopausal symptoms when you use the practice in this way for your own health. You might be surprised at how much better you feel when you work with **The Heart Alive**TM practice just to pull your sexual energy up to your heart.

If this practice can help men elongate their erection while breathing their energy up to their heart, it can certainly help women to feel more pleasure, joy and harmony when the peak of their hormones are at their rise.

After you have been doing the practice during your female cycle every month, you won't want to skip a month ever again as you discover how balanced you feel during the time you normally would feel very out of balance. Your irritability lessens. Your lethargy lessens. Your sadness turns into joy. And all other imbalances seem to disappear or lessen quite drastically. The important thing is to do the practice as soon as you notice the symptoms of the female body starting to take over. Those chemicals will run the show unless you take the whip in your own hands and tell them who's boss!

10

The Heart Alive™ and Your Kundalini

The Heart Alive™ is a practice you can use to balance the kundalini when it is out of balance, in overdrive and causing you irritability or discomfort. In moments, your sexual energy is so ignited, you feel the temptation to act on things that cause you or others difficulty, it is helpful to slow down, pause, and pull the sexual energy up to your heart. By doing this, you can self-reflect, act on things out of love instead of out of need, frustration, or anxiety.

Having a practice that forces one to slow down and go within, can be a good way to manage when your mind and body is either out of balance or in balance. It's a good navigator to determine if you're making choices from a place of balance, or a place of imbalance. It is especially helpful when other people are not ready to meet you at a place of passion, love, or connection, and they may be in deep process of their experience.

Pulling back one's heightened kundalini energy that is directed towards others can be helpful to bring love within, and decide if connecting with others is the right thing to do. It may be helpful to decide if a relationship is right for you or not, or a way to practice loving others when they do not have the same level of passion as you do. Giving others space to be with their own energy can be kind and loving and a way of showing generosity and compassion. You may discover that if your needs are not being met by the other too frequently, that they may not be the right match for you. However, practicing pulling back and self-love will be healing for you and the other, either way.

Try not to take it personally if another cannot be with your heightened sexual energy. It may have nothing to do with you and is everything about them. It may mean you are not a match, as your energies are not aligned, or you are further along

on the path of kundalini awakening than they are.
There is nothing wrong with this.

Everything comes down to choice, but choosing to
love oneself is the best choice to make. Practice
noticing your own sexual energy. If your partner(s)
cannot meet you in your sexual energy, go within
and do some deeper reflection on your inner self.
You can do this tantra meditation practice alone
then, breathe into your heart, take notice, and pull
that energy back to yourself. Pulling the sexual
energy up to your heart, putting up a boundary
around yourself, and bringing the energy into your
heart can be grounding and deeply loving to your
soul.

If you had to cut ties with someone you wanted to
be with, allow yourself time to process the energy
and feelings that show up from the slowing down
and going within. Try doing this alone before
sharing your energy with another first. The first
way to love oneself is to love oneself alone and
anchor that energy within. Then after some time,
if you choose, you can share your energy with
another again.

11

The Heart Alive™ and Sexual Trauma

For those who have had sexual trauma, **The Heart Alive™** practice is most important of all. Most people who have had sexual trauma, automatically will be living out of the sexual center for the rest of their lives, even if they are unaware of it. When someone has had sexual trauma, the root chakra, sex center will be working extra hard to try and rebalance the energy in that area.

For many it will go into extremes of need and attention. When an individual has a heightened need for sexual release after sexual trauma, this is usually a sign that there was abuse, trauma, or violation in some form. The violation that occurred in the body will try to establish a sense of equilibrium. Initially, the energy will spiral extra hard, and try to pull energy from other parts of the self to help sustain and restore its balance. The way it does this is by raising the energy and feeling the need for arousal and orgasm quite frequently.

When you know someone who has a need for sexual orgasm all the time, keep in mind this person may also have had a history of sexual trauma as well. If they claim they never had any physical sexual trauma, they may be unaware of something that happened as a young child, or there may be other things that occurred in their past.

- They may have had an angry parent, who psychically violated their boundaries often – either physically, energetically, or emotionally.

- There may be unprocessed emotions around emotional or sexual incest.

- There may be unprocessed emotions with a love relationship or sexual relationship with an adult when they were a child.

- There may be unprocessed emotions around a sexual relationship with a boyfriend or girlfriend from adolescence they didn't quite understand, or they felt violated them in some way.

After time the heightened sexual energy may go into repression. Sometimes it vacillates between sexual addictive behaviors and sexual repression and aversion behaviors. This means the energy has maintained an imbalance and they most likely will always need to work on balancing this energy — until they do some incredibly deep core work.

For some, they may just have an extended sexual aversion they think happened for no reason. They may think they are just asexual, will always be abstinent, or fear getting into a sexual relationship at all. They may not know why. This could be a family ancestral imprint they took on from their elders. It could also be from witnessing other family members who were physically or verbally abused, and they do this to protect themselves.

There also may be unprocessed emotions with someone they were in love with that didn't go anywhere, or they felt harmed them emotionally, or abandoned or rejected them in some way.

For those who have had sexual trauma, this practice of **The Heart Alive**TM is not enough, but it is a good start and a place to create awareness, and a practice of self-love to help restore the energy that has been harmed or out of balance for some time. This will be a good practice to build a sense of inner strength, inner knowing and a place to build a foundation from. For those who have had sexual trauma, you most likely will need to work with a Facilitator, to do deeper Shadow Work, and deeper core Holistic Practices to restore emotional, spiritual, and sexual balance. For those who have had sexual trauma, I recommend you read this book entirely, and do this practice for at least a couple years. It may not heal you completely, but you may find love for yourself deeper than you ever have before.

12

The Heart Alive™ as a Tantra Practice

The Heart Alive™ as a Tantra Practice is
something you can incorporate in your current
tantra practice. If you don't currently have a
tantra practice, you can start with this practice.
This is a simple meditation that can be added to
your other spiritual practices and meditation
practice. It can be a practice all on its own as well.
You can choose just to do this practice for some
time and take a break from your other practices or
add it as an additional practice to benefit from.

The important thing is to have a spiritual practice, whatever that is, and use it to help you in your personal growth, feelings of peace of mind and calming your body. You can also use your practices for personal and emotional growth. You are your best friend and your worst enemy, and you can train yourself to have a life you desire, or a life you detest.

This practice will help bring the emotional sexual energy up to your heart and merge these energies with the heart to help expand them into bliss for purification of your soul. When pulling the sexual energy up to the heart with intention, the heart becomes more aware of what it is in reaction to. Unconscious habits, patterns and behaviors become more present, and you become more aware of them.

This then allows you to become more responsible with how you show up to others and how the way you behave, feel, or think affects those in your life. You can then make more loving choices to those you care about, including yourself. As you love yourself more, others in your life will see you differently.

Your heart and your feelings about things may be more present, and they may treat you with more love in return. They may see your tenderness a little more and treat you with more respect. And those who don't treat you kinder, may become triggered by how you have changed, and start to notice it's time for them to look inward and do some of their own work.

For others who don't notice any difference, they perhaps are just not ready. That doesn't mean the work and growth you have done hasn't produced a result or an impact on others. It certainly has. But everyone is ready at their own time and their own pace.

13

The Heart Alive™ as a Yoga Practice

The Heart Alive™ as a Yoga practice is taking responsibility for your own sexuality in your everyday practice of yoga, on the mat, and off the mat. If you have an overly high sexual drive, and you enter into a yoga studio to do your practice, others around you will sense this energy. They may not say anything, but they will feel its existence.

Some people may be drawn into this energy and gravitate towards you. Others may be repulsed by this energy and try to avoid you. For others who have repressed sexual energy, sexual trauma, or a past of being overly active, it may trigger them.

As you are on the path of learning to work with raising your sexual energy up to your heart center, there will be many lessens to overcome. You will begin to look at perhaps your own repressed sexual traumas, or your own repressed sexual energy. You may look at some beliefs you've been carrying that have been holding you back from being your genuine self, or some emotional pains you have been holding deep inside your heart.

If a lot of unresolved emotions start to wake up within you, it's important to have a loving partner or guide to help assist you to release the emotions that are surfacing. The sections in this book on doing the practice in a relationship and marriage will help with this. I recommend reading this whole document, and if you need help, seek out help. It can be overwhelming to do this work alone, and you certainly will learn more about yourself and grow more when you have someone to support you by your side.

The more aware you are of your sexual energy, and the more responsible you are to transform it, the more it will grow to becoming integrated into your whole self, rather than lying dormant in your root center. You will feel more love for yourself and others. You will see the truth of others and their genuineness. And you will live more from a place of love in the world.

The more we can transform from lower frequencies of heightened sexual addictive or obsessive energies, the more we will find our innocence, and our *inner child* will be healed, whole and complete.

For those who have been overly active in the past and turned it off, you may be surprised at the heightened sexual energy within you that begins to awaken. For those of you with this experience, it's important not to judge yourself and not to be afraid. Its ok that you had strong sexual energy in the past, and its ok if it is resurfacing again. Now you know you have control over it. And perhaps now is your time to heal it and take a look at it deeper.

14

The Heart Alive™ in Your Meditation Practice

You can use **The Heart Alive™** practice in your meditation practice to lift your energy up higher, help ground sexual energy that is already very high, help open and heal the heart, help connect deeper to self-love and also loving your partner deeper. You can use the practice in your meditation practice for whatever intention that suits you best. What your needs are, and your current goals can help dictate how you manage and work with your own energy. How you control your energy, redirect it, and channel your energy will be the main component as to how to use the practice to support you.

The practice of channeling the energy up to the heart, can be done as a practice for activating and awakening, or to help settle high energy and feel more grounded and integrated into yourself. If the intention is to feel more sexual energy and bring it up to the heart, when you already feel high sexual energy currently, it may in fact expand your heart chakra without even knowing it. It can potentially cause a heart orgasm, and an experience of bliss throughout the body. Emotions may surface you did not know were there.

If you do your practice with the intention of grounding your sexual energy, it will help assist to settle energy that may be out of control. If you attempt to do the practice to help open repressed and shut down sexual energy, it may also help lift lethargic energy, or a form of what they call depression, or low energy, and awaken a feeling of self-love that brings more peace to the body. You will not know how it affects you until after you attempt to do the practice for several weeks and especially after months.

Intention is the most important thing when doing this practice.

Where your mind goes, energy flows. So, direct the energy to what you need and want, and you reap the rewards.

15

The Heart Alive™ in Your Breathwork Practice

The Heart Alive™ practice during your expanded Kriya, or Conscious Connected Breathwork Practice, is done while you do your Breathwork practice, sitting upright or laying down. Every Breathwork practice is done with intention of what you want to work on, how you want to focus the energy and what you want to let go of. When the intention is to work with your sexual energy, and in this case raising the root chakra energy up to the heart center, you will discover what your breath helps to assist in transforming.

Each Breathwork practice with this intention will be a little more powerful than with simple focus and meditation. The breathing will be deeper, more expansive, more powerful and has an opportunity to move the energy that much stronger. You may feel a heart orgasm on the first practice or an emotional release on the first practice, or it may take a few sessions. The opportunity with doing the practice during your breathwork practice is to go deeper within, having even less distractions, more of an opportunity to go into the practice and having more results as well.

Again, one will not know the benefits of this work without doing the actual practice on a consistent or regular basis. It will take time, commitment, and dedication, but the rewards will multiply with each session you experience.

How To Do **The Heart Alive**TM Practice During a Breathwork Session

Set up and prepare to do your normal Breathwork Practice. Wherever is your favorite place to breathe, set up this area for your spiritual healing. If you use music with your breathwork, do the same thing as you usually do.

Set your intention of what you want to let go of, and what you want to release and transform. When you are ready, get into a relaxed position, and start your breathing practice. While you are laying down or sitting upright and doing your deep circular breathing in and out of the mouth, focus your attention on the root center on your inhale, and bring your attention on the heart area on the exhale. Continue the circular breathing in and out of the mouth, deep breaths in and long breaths out.

All you need to do is focus on your breathing. The body will do the rest. As you melt deeper into the practice, you will discover what feelings arise, and what feelings are stuck. Just continue the intention of breathing in a circular way, and the body will do the rest. Continue the intention of breathing into the root area on the inhale and bringing the exhale up to the heart. Watch as magic happens!

Be sure to wear an eye mask, and have a blanket nearby. Make sure you use the restroom before you start, and turn off any sounds from any devices that might distract you from your process. Surrender, and let go!

16

The Heart Alive™ to Awaken a Sleepy Sex Drive

When one has a sex drive that has all but turned off, usually there is an emotional reason behind this repression. Sometimes it is chemical and physical, but most often it is emotional and spiritual. In this section, we're going to talk about waking up sexual energy that has disappeared and given up on you.

Perhaps you gave up on yourself a long time ago. Perhaps your feelings have been hurt too many times and you kept your feelings to yourself, or your partner didn't give you a chance to express your feelings to them. Perhaps too, you never shared your feelings with anyone else either. Or, maybe you didn't say everything that was needed to be said, and a lot of feelings, thoughts and emotions have been stuffed. This often happens in long term relationships, where relationships ended without a resolution or conclusion.

Doing this practice to help assist in re-activating your sex drive is just as important as it is for those who have a high drive and need to tame it or calm it down.

Repressed feelings and emotions can lay dormant in the body for years. Until one has released all the past pains, emotions and energies trapped in the body, mind and cells, one can remain stagnant and repressed for the rest of their life. It is a choice to let things go, and most often we cannot do it alone.

We can fill up the void of the pain from past lovers with a new lover, but you'll only be repeating the same patterns and history as before. When you can truly work on the deep energies trapped in the body will one be able to be free of their past and be free to feel sexy and juicy in their body again.

You have to do the work, the deep work, and go to your core, your center. When you can be honest with yourself and honest with others about what you endured in past love relationships and express everything about all of it completely will you then get a chance to be free.

Often, we carry the emotions of old relationships in our body. And we can carry the energy of the emotions anywhere on our body. It can be inside the muscles of the lower back, the mid back, the shoulders, the neck, the deep groin area, inside the genitals, in the stomach area and inside the heart. We can also carry the energy in our throats and anywhere else. Doing **The Heart Alive**™ practice to awaken the stuck energy in the body will bring consciousness to areas that have been asleep.

As layers of different emotions arise, it's important to be gentle with yourself and extremely patient. At first it may feel like the practice is not working. Feelings of anger, frustration or resentment may surface at first. As those layers are processed and released, eventually you may go deeper and deeper into the self and start to get in touch with feelings of longing, disappointment, sadness, loss, and heartache. When you continue the practice, you may get a chance to process grief hidden within.

It may be helpful to journal as layers of emotions arise. It may be helpful to have a therapist or counselor to talk to. It may also be helpful to do a yoga practice to help release the emotions in the body. And maintain a gentle mindfulness meditation practice to help with keeping grounded, centered, and balanced as you work through all the layers of the self.

The Heart Alive™ practice to awaken a dormant sexual life, sexual energy and vitality is truly possible. Doing it for this intention does take work and deep commitment. But in time, your heart will be healed. Your body will be freer. And you will feel sexually alive and blissful in your body again.

17

The Heart Alive™ as part of Your Grief Work

When you're going through the experience of grieving a loved one, sometimes the sexual energy can raise high after interacting with others before you are ready to experience intimacy. If you're loved one was a significant partner, husband, wife or intimate, and your sexual energy is high with a new person right away, it may in fact be your emotional body that needs to heal. Sharing sexual energy with a new person before you are ready would be discouraged. It is best to wait until you are fully processed from the grief of your loved one before starting a new intimate relationship.

Sometimes, on the journey of transformation, grieving any aspect of your past may show up. It would be important to your partner to be supportive of your grieving process and help assist you in this experience. If you have a sexual relationship with someone and you are also on the journey of awakening, it is natural to sometimes go through a grieving process. Being supportive of each other's process would create a healthy relationship.

If you were in a relationship prior to the death of a loved one, and the relationship is already established, it would be important to the partner of the one going through the grieving to be as supportive as possible. The partner of the one grieving does need support as well, and their needs to be met, but in order to maintain the love with each other, it would be best to hold the container for their partner as much as possible and not to take their lack of sexual drive personally or make it about themselves.

Sometimes it can be quite a challenge for the partner of the one who lost a loved one. For the partner of the one who lost a loved one, they too need to know they are loved. For those individuals, doing this practice is just as important as the one who lost someone, perhaps even more so. This would be an opportunity for you to truly practice being of service and learn to be detached from how your partner feels, behaves, or reacts. For those who are the partners, this is your opportunity to truly evolve and transform as a person. If you can maintain loving your partner who suffered the loss, your relationship will blossom that much more. This is a great opportunity to do this practice together. You both then get to work through the emotions of the heart, feel deeper in yourselves at your core, and build a closer relationship with each other than ever before.

From the book Grieving the Shamans Way:

CHANNELING SEXUAL ENERGY AND BRINGING IT TO THE HEART

When your sexual energy is so high how do you bring it to the heart? It's important to bring the energy up to the heart when you're feeling so much energy in your body and you know that it needs to come from a place of love. It's time to bring that love energy and raise it up to your heart. Your own energy is your teacher. It is your guide. It is a message to go inward. We can have energy that's really strong but when it's so strong it's looking outside, it's time to bring it inward and see it as a teacher.

How do you bring your energy up to your heart? First, it's about noticing and then after you notice it go within. Take that energy and pull it up to your heart and center yourself.

How do you pull the energy up to your heart? The first step is to notice that your sexual energy is extremely high.

If your sexual energy is mixed with high emotions that are difficult to deal with, the important thing to do is notice those emotions. If you have anger, it is imperative to process the anger. If you have grief, it is crucial to process the grief. If you feel resentment, disappointment, confusion, animosity, or any emotion where you would be projecting unloving feelings, thoughts, or behaviors onto another, the first thing to do is to become balanced within the self-first. You don't want to be putting those feelings onto other people, and especially someone you care about, or have an interest in getting close to. I talk about how you can process anger and other emotions throughout this book.

For now, we're going to go over how you can channel your sexual energy up to your heart. Once, you feel clear of any unhealthy or dark emotions, then you can channel the positive energies and emotions up to your heart.

Practice on Channeling Sexual Energy and Bringing it to Your Heart

Step 1: Start with your Breath

Do deep belly breathing, where you inhale in your nose, and exhale out your mouth. When you inhale in your nose, pull the breath fully into your belly. Let your belly expand fully as though it is sticking out from eating a full meal, or the analogy I like to use, "Like Santa

Clause." Start with a count of 4 or 5, and then tilt your pelvis forward about 1 to 2 inches while squeezing your kegel muscles at the same time. The goal is to eventually squeeze the genital muscles from your anus to your inner reproductive system (where you would hold your pee if you had to urinate).

After you squeeze these muscles, again, you want to hold for a count of 4 to 6, and then as you exhale, instead of exhaling the breath down the legs to raise your sexual energy or ground your energy, you want to visualize the breath going up to your heart center. As the breath is going up, your pelvis returns to normal position. Bring the breath directly to the center of your heart chakra at your breastbone area. As the energy comes to this region you should be fully at the end of your exhale.

Step 2: Continue Breathing in this Way

Now, you want to continue to breathe in this way, inhaling and exhaling in this circular manner. Continue the movement in your pelvis and hips. Continue the squeezing and relaxing practice. If your mind starts to wander or tries to, bring it back with your attention to your breath, and your disciplined practice of this breathing method.

Step 3: Continue this Process for 15 minutes to a half an Hour

When first starting this practice, set the timer. You can start with 10 minutes and work your way up to a half an hour or longer. The more you practice this technique, the easier it becomes. Your muscles will get stronger. Your mind will have an easier time to focus on the practice. And as soon as you recognize your sexual energy is charged, you'll know what to do.

Step 4: Continue your personal work

If there are any other emotions that arise during this process, and it is too difficult to sit with or be with, certainly you can ask for help. You may also want to journal. If it is uncomfortable, you can get up and do some Somatic Movement, shaking, dancing, making sounds of expression or releasing anger or frustration.

Step 5: Putting your Practice to Good Use

After you've been doing this practice for a while, you can invite a partner to do the practice with you or seek consultation or healing with a practitioner to help you. If you struggle to maintain self-control when with a partner, it is important to seek a professional to help assist you. The key here is pulling your sexual energy up to your heart. After you have been doing this practice for some time, and you still are left with an enormous amount of sexual energy, and tons of unprocessed and difficult emotions, it may be a good time to find a practitioner to support you to process these emotions.

Step 6: How to Process Big Emotions that are Trapped in Your Root (or Second) Chakra

If you are feeling a high degree of need to connect to another sexually, and you know you still have more grief work to do or have a large amount of unprocessed anger in your body, it is important to seek help to process these feelings. Sometimes we can project these emotions onto our partners without knowing it, and it can hurt or harm a relationship. Some people, and perhaps many, have obsessive or sexually addictive behaviors and are unaware of this. The root of addiction or obsession is a longing for love that was never received as a young child when we most needed it. To rebalance our emotional and energetic system, it's important to be aware of this, acknowledge it, communicate to those we are interacting with that this is present, and ask for help.

18

The Heart Alive™ and Ascension

The Heart Alive™ and Ascension is a path that takes one towards ascension as they acknowledge all their feelings and take responsibility for all parts of themselves. Spiritual growth is only successful when emotional and psychological growth can be awakened and maintained. Ascension is a journey of awakening, and evolving the whole self, from all levels and layers of who you are.

The Heart Alive™ as a path to Ascension is a practice of awakening the whole self and continually doing the deep work until transformation is attainable and possible. We all must continue to do our personal growth and take responsibility for how we show up in the world, how we behave, react, respond, and interact with the world around us. In order to achieve true growth as an individual we have to look at all the shadow parts of the self, even the parts we don't know that exist.

Many see Ascension as just an advanced version of spirituality, but it encompasses all aspects of transformation of the entire self, the entire physical body, the entire spiritual self and the entire soul. It is a journey into the unknown of who you are, who you were before, and who you aspire to be. Transformation of the emotional self in fact takes much more work than any other aspect of the self. When emphasis is solely on the spiritual practices creating bliss, euphoria, connection to spirit, and opening of the energy body, it can sometimes bypass important shadow work. The emotional body and hidden feelings within that need to be acknowledged, dealt with, processed, and transformed are at the precipice of transformation of the whole self where the possibility of Ascension lives.

19

The Heart Alive™ and Plant Medicine

One of the most powerful practices one can do is merging and blending the beautiful practices of Breathwork and Plant Medicine. Often Plant Medicine will trigger the body to breathing deeper than it does in normal states and causes the body to breathe in areas of the body that are holding tension, emotional energy, and trauma to be released. When combining Plant Medicine with the advanced practice of **The Heart Alive™** style of breathing, one can access deeper parts of blocks to energies that are keeping their bodies, heart or soul stuck or unresolved related to their sexuality, sensuality, and intimacy.

We are at a change in history, where more people on the planet than ever are seeking and searching for ways to develop their spirituality and advance as humans. More people than ever are becoming Healers, Practitioners and Coaches for personal growth. Yoga is old news and Breathwork, Sound Healing and Plant Medicine are the new popular practices today.

Many people are looking for ways to evolve and genuinely want to grow and become better. Self-education is more popular than ever, and many look for real solutions to their problems and ways of expanding themselves. This Meditation & Breathwork practice of **The Heart Alive**™ combined with Plant Medicine is one of the most powerful ways of transforming and evolving the self. No matter what choice of medicine you work with, in particular, the natural medicines that come from the Earth, combining it with this practice of breathing will bring you closer to God, your inner soul, your inner core and the truth of all of who you are than anything imaginable.

When your intention to work with entheogenic and psychedelic plant medicine is to become a better person, heal your true self, and cause transformation, combining it with a practice of deep breathing meditation is a perfect match.

112

Wholeness is met with love! Medicine is met with deeper ease, understanding and peace!

Having a regular practice of breathwork and breathing in this way will make all other experiences in life that much more powerful and beautiful. Being able to breathe fully in and take profound breaths makes everything more magical. And when combining this practice with plant medicine it allows the power of the medicine to do what it does normally at an even more significant level, because it doesn't have to work as hard when you know how to work with it.

Your body surrenders deeper into the medicine. There is less resistance to work with and an easier time to let go, melt, and surrender into what the medicine is showing you. Holding on to what no longer serves you, old habits, challenging feelings, and beliefs, and fighting with the self during moments of deep process lessens and acceptance becomes easier. The ability to relax and allow the healing process to occur becomes more natural, accessible, and truly possible.

Gaining and having the ability to do **The Heart Alive**™ breathing practice, or any Breathwork practice for that matter, during your deep dive into the unknown of profound and beautiful Plant & Earth Medicine work, you will be less in the mind, and more embodied to experience all of yourself. Your whole body will feel what it needs to feel and experience in order to have a profound awakening and transforming experience.

20

The Heart Alive™ as a Continued Practice for Humanity to Evolve

Maintaining the practice of **The Heart Alive™** in Meditation and Breathwork as a practice for humanity to grow has the opportunity for the community as a whole to evolve. There are many practices and modalities, tools, and more ways of expanding consciousness than ever before. This breathing practice, for the individuals of our planet who are stuck living out of the sex center, have imbalances in their sex center, a history of sexual trauma, or psychic sexual trauma gives the humans who are living today an opportunity to grow and heal, which is almost everyone.

Everyone has something to work through when it comes to love, intimacy, relationships, and sexuality. Often those who don't know they have something to work through in these areas have more to heal than those who do. Many who are actively working on these things often come up short and feel stuck, stopped, and don't know how to progress or have life show up differently or more beautiful. They may have succeeded to a certain degree and come so far, but don't know how to advance further along in their journey and make it remarkable. They may have given up, or just accepted things the way they are. Perhaps they don't believe it can get any better.

For those who truly do the work, and want to accomplish all the goals, possibilities and achieve all this practice has to offer, miracles will unfold. And you will be ever surprised at all the gifts you will receive.

Sometimes one has to take a step back from their life, go into silence, and be alone for some time. This may be the path to take you to the next level. And for others, they may be gifted the opportunity to advance along this path with a Beloved in their arms. Life is constantly changing. There are many ups and downs and lessons to learn. We're all here for the ride. Let's make it the most enjoyable possible and the best life could ever offer…By feeling your true self, being your true self, and letting the best you shine!

Resources

The Miracle of the Breath, Mastering Fear, Healing Illness, and Experiencing the Divine, by Andy Caponigro

Holotropic Breathwork, A New Approach to Self-Exploration and Therapy, by Stanislav Grof & Christina Grof

Shamanic Breathwork, Journey Beyond the Limits of the Self, by Linda Star Wolf

Breath by Breath, The Liberating Practice of Insight Meditation, by Larry Rosenberg, with David Guy

The Future of Love, The Power of the Soul in Intimate Relationships, by Daphne Rose Kingma

The Awakening of Kundalini, by Gopi Krishna

The Seven Levels of Intimacy, The Art of Loving and the Joy of Being Loved, by Matthew Kelly

Hold Me Tight, Seven Conversations for a Lifetime of Love, by Dr Sue Johnson

Wrestling with Love, How Men Struggle with Intimacy, by Samuel Osherson, PhD

Loving Your Partner without Losing Yourself, by Martha Baldwin Beveridge

Getting the Love You Want, A Guide for Couples, by Harville Hendrix, PhD

Embracing the Beloved, Relationship as a path of Awakening, by Stephen and Ondrea Levine

Receiving Love, Transform your Relationship by Letting Yourself be Loved, by Harville Hendrix, PhD & Helen Lakelly Hunt, PhD

Intimacy, Trusting Oneself and the Other, by Osho

Chakras and Their Archetypes, Uniting Energy, Awareness and Spiritual Growth, by Ambika Wauters

Dreaming Wide Awake, Lucid Dreaming, Shamanic Healing, and Psychedelics, by David Jay Brown

Psychedelic Healing, The Promise of Entheogens for Psychotherapy and Spiritual Development, by Neal M Goldsmith, PhD

San Pedro, The Gateway to Wisdom, Shamanic Plant Medicine, by Ross Heaven

Psychedelic Psychotherapy, A User Friendly Guide to Psychedelic Drug Assisted Psychotherapy, R Coleman

How to Change Your Mind, What the New Science of Psychedelics Teaches Us About Consciousness, Dying, Addiction, Depression, and Transcendence, by Michael Pollan

Transforming the Mind, Teachings on Generating Compassion, His Holiness the Dalai Lama

Sexual Anorexia, Overcoming Sexual Self Hatred, by Patrick Carnes, PhD

Sex and Love Addicts Anonymous, First Edition, The Augustine Fellowship

Sex Addicts Anonymous, From Shame to Grace, International Organization of SAA

Articles from the Journal, Stories with a Healthy Relationship Focus, The Augustine Fellowship

Meeting the Shadow, The Hidden Power of the Dark Side of Human Nature, Edited by Connie Zweig and Jeremiah Abrams

Energies of Transformation, A Guide to the Kundalini Process, by Bonnie Greenwell PhD

Frequency, The Power of Personal Vibration, by Penny Peirce

Sex for One, The Joy of Self Loving, by Betty Dodson, PhD

Becoming Orgasmic, A Sexual and Personal Growth Program for Women, by Julia R Heiman, PhD & Joseph LoPiccolo, PhD

Womb Wisdom, Awakening the Creative and Forgotten Powers of the Feminine, by Padma and Anaiya Aon Prakasha

After Silence, Rape & My Journey Back, by Nancy Venable Raine

The Unsayable, The Hidden Language of Trauma, by Annie G Rogers, PhD

Glossary

Ascension – *noun*, the act of ascending, ascent.
The Ascension, the bodily ascending of Christ from earth to heaven. Ascend - to move, climb, or go upward; mount; rise. Ascension in this context is the act of moving towards enlightenment, and achieving higher states of consciousness, frequency and advancing oneself as a human.

Awakening – the act of awakening, a revival of interest of attention. Rousing, quickening. In the context of spiritual development, awakening is the act of pursuit in spiritual growth and development towards the path of ascension.

Blocks – in the context of spiritual growth or the physical body, a block is an area of obstruction keeping someone stuck or trapped in the past. It may be an energetic blockage, an emotional blockage, a spiritual block, or something hidden from someone's view and their ability to see behind it. It may keep someone from seeing the truth or reality of what is so.

Breathwork – Breathwork as described throughout this book, is a spiritual holistic practice of breathing deeply in the body for emotional, spiritual, or physical healing. It is a practice of becoming consciously aware of one's own breath, and using the breath for personal growth and development.

Chakras – in yoga, any of the seven major energy center of the body. In Ascension teachings, the chakras can go higher than 200 energy centers going all throughout the body, all the way up to the higher realms in the sky beyond the clouds, and all the way below the body down to the core of the earth.

Channeling – in the context of bodywork, or body scanning, channeling here is the practice of intentionally visualizing energy throughout the body to direct it in a certain way or intuitively get a sense of the energy and which way it is being directed.

Chemical Imbalances – Chemical Imbalances caused by Hormones is the medical definition of Hormonal imbalances, which occur when there is too much or too little of a hormone in the blood. Symptoms depend on which hormone is out of balance and the person's natal sex. Common symptoms include weight changes, lower sex drive, and acne. Hormones are chemicals produced by glands in the endocrine system.

Conscious Connected Breathwork - Conscious Connected Breathwork is a circular breath technique. This means that inhalations are immediately followed by exhalations without pause. When maintained for upwards of an hour, Conscious Connected Breathwork brings on non-ordinary states of consciousness and can lead to profound experiences of healing.

Energy Frequency - Energy is the life force that flows through all things. It is the source of our power and the key to creating anything we desire. Frequency is the rate at which energy vibrates. This can be measured in hertz (Hz). Vibration is the amplitude, or intensity, of energy.

Entheogens - Entheogens are psychoactive substances that induce alterations in perception, mood, consciousness, cognition, or behavior for the purposes of engendering spiritual development or otherwise in sacred contexts.

Frequency - The frequency of free vibration is known as free or natural frequency. Whenever a body is set into vibrations, then in absence of any externally impressed force upon it, the body will go on vibrating with a characteristic frequency of its own.

Heart Center – The heart center is another name for the heart chakra. It is the area at the center of the chest that radiates the energy of love out and receives the energy from love from others and from the self.

Inner Child - In popular psychology and analytical psychology, the inner child is an individual's childlike aspect. It includes what a person learned as a child, before puberty. The inner child is often conceived as a semi-independent subpersonality subordinate to the waking conscious mind.

It's a valuable concept from psychology, and it refers to the childlike part of your unconscious mind. Many trace the concept of an inner child back to psychiatrist Carl Jung. Essentially, our inner child is the forgiving, free-spirited part of us that still feels and experiences life as a child.

Inner Wisdom – Inner wisdom is the guidance that comes from within ourselves. It is a connection to our personal truth and an inherent inner knowing of our path in life. Accessing inner wisdom can be achieved through quiet reflection, meditation, or simply by tuning into your inner thoughts and feelings.

Inner Wisdom is what is referred to as someone's inner knowing about the world and themselves. It is a place to stand from and believe in themselves.

Internal Wounds - The wounds your inner child suffers are essentially scars and trauma sites that never healed on your inner hopeful self. These scars are the result of painful experiences and treatment by others. Instead of processing these and healing, you simply keep mentally picking at the scabs and making it bleed.

Kriya – is a "completed action", technique or practice within a yoga discipline meant to achieve a specific result. Kriya or Kriya Yoga may also refer to: Kriya Yoga school, a modern yoga school. Kriya, a class of Tantra in Tibetan Buddhism.

Kriya is the path of action; also involuntary body movement caused by the regular or increased flow of pranic energy.

Kundalini - Kundalini is the term for "a spiritual energy or life force located at the base of the spine", conceptualized as a coiled-up serpent. The practice of Kundalini yoga is supposed to arouse the sleeping Kundalini Shakti from its coiled base through the 6 chakras, and penetrate the 7th chakra, or crown.

Meditation – Meditation is a practice in which an individual uses a technique – such as mindfulness, or focuses the mind on a particular object, thought, or activity – to train attention and awareness, and achieve a mentally clear and emotionally calm and stable state.

Meditation is practiced in numerous religious traditions. The earliest records of meditation (dhyana) are found in the Upanishads, and meditation plays a salient role in the contemplative repertoire of Hinduism, Jainism and Buddhism. Since the 19th century, Asian meditative techniques have spread to other cultures where they have also found application in non-spiritual contexts, such as business and health.

Meditation may significantly reduce stress, anxiety, depression, and pain, and enhance peace, perception, self-concept, and well-being. Research is ongoing to better understand the effects of meditation on health (psychological, neurological, and cardiovascular) and other areas.

Romantic Obsessions - Despite its name, romantic obsession is pretty much the opposite of love. With its roots in the darker side of human behavior, it is much more like an addiction than anything else.
When we obsess over a romantic partner, we essentially put that person on a pedestal and won't let them come down. We make them more important than us, while also setting that important person up to let us down in the long run. (Huffpost.com)

Plant Medicine - There are a few ways to approach the definition of plant medicines. The most straightforward of which is simply looking at two words that make up this term.

By "plants," most individuals are referring to an organic, unadulterated substance that is naturally occurring. And "medicine" refers to possessing medicinal qualities that help individuals heal from illnesses and ailments, whether physical or psychological in nature.

Common examples of plant medicines include mushrooms, ayahuasca, and 5-MEO-DMT from the Bufo Alvarius toad. All of these substances are made with natural plant or animal ingredients, are not synthesized in a lab, and are taken in their raw, unaltered form.

It's important to note that plant medicines don't need to be psychoactive or psychedelic in nature. Tea is arguably the most ancient plant medicine, with its use in healing illnesses spanning back thousands of years.

However, in the context of psychedelics and plant medicines, people often point to natural compounds that also exhibit psychedelic properties.

An opposite to plant medicine would be something like LSD, which requires complex synthesis in a lab to create, and cannot be harvested or found in nature. (mindbloom.com)

Self-love - the instinct by which one's actions are directed to the promotion of one's own welfare or well-being, especially an excessive regard for one's own advantage.
conceit; vanity.

Sex Addiction - Sex addiction refers to excessive sexual thoughts, desires, urges or behaviors that can't be controlled and cause distress and harm to your relationships, finances, and other aspects of your life. Sexual addiction is also called hypersexuality, compulsive sexual behavior and other names. Treatments include medications, psychotherapy, and self-help support groups.

Sex Center – Sex Center is another name for the Root Chakra, and area dominated by ones sexual organs located on the body.

Sexual Arousal - Arousal is the feeling of being turned on sexually. When you're turned on, your body experiences physical and emotional changes. Your penis or clitoris may get erect (hard), engorged, and sensitive, and you may feel wetness on your vulva or vagina, or on the tip of your penis.

Sexual Energy - Sexual energy at its most basic level is the driving force behind the sexual act itself. It is linked to both innate biological programs as well as our desires. Your sexual energy is a life-giving energy which is sustaining and maintaining you all the time.

Sexual Repression - Sexual repression occurs when a person prevents themselves from feeling/experiencing natural sexual urges and desires. 1. A sexually repressed person will usually hold negative ideas towards sex. This person may consider the act, and everything associated with it, wrong.

Sexual Tension - Sexual tension occurs when two individuals interact and feel sexual desire, yet no sexual activity happens. Sexual tension is more about everything leading up to sex than the actual act of having sex.

Sexual Trauma - sexual trauma refers to one or multiple sexual violations that invoke significant distress. The term sexual trauma is used based on clinical observations that some survivors do not label their experiences as rape or assault due to familiarity with the perpetrator or the absence of force.

Sexual Urges – When it comes to sexual urges, this is the desire to respond to a sexual craving in the body. Sexual urges is characterized by lust, sexuality, sexual desire, sex drive and passion.

Sexual Vitality – sexual vitality is the level of energy of your sexual libido.

Tantra - (/'tæntrə/; Sanskrit: तन्त्र, lit. 'expansion-device, salvation-spreader; loom, weave, warp') refers to an esoteric yogic tradition that developed on the Indian subcontinent from the middle of the 1st millennium CE onwards in both Hinduism and Buddhism.

The term tantra, in the Indian traditions, also means any systematic broadly applicable "text, theory, system, method, instrument, technique or practice". A key feature of these traditions is the use of mantras, and thus they are commonly referred to as Mantramārga ("Path of Mantra") in Hinduism or Mantrayāna ("Mantra Vehicle") and Guhyamantra ("Secret Mantra") in Buddhism.

Trauma - Trauma is a pervasive problem. It results
from exposure to an incident or series of events that are
emotionally disturbing or life-threatening with lasting
adverse effects on the individual's functioning and
mental, physical, social, emotional, and/or spiritual
well-being.

Yoga - Yoga (/ˈjoʊɡə/;[1] Sanskrit: योग, lit. 'yoke' or
'union' pronounced [joːɡɐ]) is a group of physical,
mental, and spiritual practices or disciplines which
originated in ancient India and aim to control (yoke)
and still the mind, recognizing a detached witness-
consciousness untouched by the mind (Chitta) and
mundane suffering (Duḥkha). There is a wide variety of
schools of yoga, practices, and
goals in Hinduism, Buddhism, and Jainism, and
traditional and modern yoga is practiced worldwide.

About the Author

Asttarte Deva, aka, Jennifer Rose, is a leading expert on Spiritual Healing, Tantra, Holistic Therapies, and has spent her life in the discovery and on the transformation of herself, and is dedicated to sharing her wisdom, knowledge, and experience to others. In all of her writings, she shares her experience in Vibrational Therapy, Reiki, Yoga, Meditation, Breathwork, Holistic Healing and Health. She also shares her experience as a Tantra Teacher, Healer & Life Coach. Asttarte's multiple styles and eclectic immersion of Psychotherapy modalities, Bodywork, and experience and development with Spirit Medicines, Psychedelics, Trauma and Grief makes her a living example of someone who has walked through the journey herself.

She has a private practice where she offers sessions, but her main focus is on her writing, teaching, group events and retreats.

Asttarte has been a practitioner in the Healing Arts most of her life, and as an adult became Certified and Trained in multiple styles of Reiki, Massage, Yoga, Tantra, Life & Transformational Coaching, Breathwork, Relationship Coaching, Sex & Intimacy and has an innate intuitive wisdom she has carried with her entire life. In her more current years, she has trained under the knowledge and guidance of multiple types of Shamans and Spirit Medicine Facilitators and now combines this wisdom with her previous work in the Healing Arts. She has also been a Writer most of her life, and she hopes you will use these volumes as guides on your journey. May they serve you, bring you knowledge and wisdom and help you on the path of your own discovery and enlightenment.

Asttarte is also the Author of Awaken to Living, Tantra for Your Whole Life, The Heart On, Opening the Heart of Your Beloved & Grieving the Shamans Way, What I Learned from the Love of My Life Dying, On Healing the Shadow Side of a Relationship After your Greatest Loss, With the Wisdom of Bufo the Toad, Spirit Medicine, Tantra, Intimacy, Breathwork & Being Our Authentic Selves and Grieving the Shamans Way Handbook.

To reach Asttarte, go to her Shamanic, Couples and Tantra Coaching site at AsttarteDeva.com, and her Energy Frequency Healing site at CenterforHealingArts.net

www.ingramcontent.com/pod-product-compliance
Lightning Source LLC
LaVergne TN
LVHW052031080426
835513LV00018B/2266